A COLLECTION
OF JOY

HELEN STEINER RICE

BARBOUR
PUBLISHING

A HELEN STEINER RICE ® Product

© 2011 by Barbour Publishing, Inc.

ISBN 978-1-61626-204-4

Published by Barbour Publishing, Inc., P.O. Box 719, Uhrichsville, Ohio 44683, www.barbourbooks.com

Our mission is to publish and distribute inspirational products offering exceptional value and biblical encouragement to the masses.

ecpa Member of the
Evangelical Christian
Publishers Association

Printed in the United States of America.

CONTENTS

JOYFUL
OCCASIONS

A New Year's Meditation

What better time and what better season,
What greater occasion or more wonderful reason
To kneel down in prayer and lift our hands high
To the God of creation, who made earth and sky,
Who sent us His Son to live here among men —
And the message He brought is
as true now as then. . .
So at this glad season, when there's joy everywhere,
Let us meet our Redeemer at the altar of prayer,
Asking Him humbly to bless all of our days
And grant us forgiveness for our erring ways. . .
And though we're unworthy, dear Father above,
Accept us today and let us dwell in Thy love
So we may grow stronger upheld by Thy grace,
And with Thy assistance be ready to face
All the temptations that fill every day,
And hold on to our hands when
we stumble and stray. . .
And thank You, dear God, for the
year that now ends
And for the great blessing of
loved ones and friends.

WORDS CAN SAY SO LITTLE

Today is an occasion for compliments and praise
And saying many of the things
we don't say other days.
For often through the passing days
we feel deep down inside
Unspoken thoughts of thankfulness
and fond, admiring pride.
But words can say so little when
the heart is overflowing,
And often those we love the most
just have no way of knowing
The many things the heart conceals
and never can impart,
For words seem so inadequate to
express what's in the heart.

REASON TO CELEBRATE

"Let not your heart be troubled"—
Let not your soul be sad.
Easter is a time of joy
When all hearts should be glad—
Glad to know that Jesus Christ
Made it possible for men
To have their sins forgiven
And, like Him, to live again. . .
So at this joyous season
May the wondrous Easter story
Renew our faith so we may be
Partakers of His glory.

Today's Joy Was Born
of Yesterday's Sorrow

Who said the darkness of the
night would never turn to day?
Who said the winter's bleakness
would never pass away?
Who said the fog would never
lift and let the sunshine through?
Who said the skies, now overcast,
would nevermore be blue?
Why should we ever entertain
these thoughts so dark and grim
And let the brightness of our
minds grow cynical and dim
When we know beyond all questioning
that winter turns to spring
And on the notes of sorrow
new songs are made to sing?
For no one sheds a teardrop
or suffers loss in vain,
For God is always there to
turn our losses into gain. . .
And every burden borne today
and every present sorrow
Are but God's happy harbingers
of a joyous, bright tomorrow.

BIRTHDAYS ARE A GIFT FROM GOD

Where does time go in its endless flight?
Spring turns to fall and day to night,
And birthdays come and birthdays go,
And where they go we do not know. . .
But God, who planned our life on earth
And gave our minds and bodies birth,
And then enclosed a living soul
With heaven as the spirit's goal,
Has given man the gift of choice
To follow that small inner voice
That speaks to us from year to year,
Reminding us we've naught to fear. . .
For birthdays are a stepping stone
To endless joys as yet unknown—
So fill each day with happy things,
And may your burdens all take wing
And fly away and leave behind
Great joy of heart and peace of mind. . .
For birthdays are the gateway to
An endless life of joy for you
If you but pray from day to day
That He will show you the truth and the way.

Happy Memories

Birthdays come and birthdays go
And with them come the thought
Of all the happy memories
The passing years have brought,
And looking back across the years
We come to recognize
That it takes a lot of birthdays
To make us kind and wise,
For growing older only means
The spirit grows serene
And we behold things with our souls
That our eyes have never seen.
For each birthday is a gateway
That leads to a reward,
The rich reward of learning
- The true greatness of the Lord.

For a Young Person at Confirmation

When we are confirmed in our faith in the Lord,
Our greatest possession and richest reward
Is knowing that now we are heralds of the King,
Ready His praises and glory to sing. . .
And oh, what a privilege to witness for God
And to walk in the way that the dear Savior trod—
Confirmed in the faith that we are
upheld by His hand,
Eager to follow His smallest command,
Secure in the knowledge that though now and then
We're guilty of sins that are common to men,
He freely forgives and understands, too,
And there's nothing—no, nothing
that God cannot do. . .
And great is our gladness to serve
Him through others,
For our Father taught us that all men are brothers,
And the people we meet on life's thoroughfares
Are burdened with trouble and sorrow and cares,
And this is the chance we are given each day
To witness for God and to try to obey
His laws and commandments and
to make our Confirmation
A service of joy and a real dedication.

$\mathcal{W}$HAT IS MARRIAGE?

It is sharing and caring,
Giving and forgiving,
Loving and being loved,
Walking hand in hand,
Talking heart to heart,
Seeing through each other's eyes,
Laughing together,
Weeping together,
Praying together,
And always trusting and believing
And thanking God for each other. . .
For love that is shared is a beautiful thing—
It enriches the soul and makes the heart sing.

*W*HAT IS A BABY?

A baby is a gift of life born of the wonder of love—
A little bit of eternity sent from the Father above,
Giving a new dimension to the love
between husband and wife
And putting an added new meaning
to the wonder and mystery of life.

*P*EACE

May we never forget those who sleep 'neath the sod
They helped liberate, by the grace of our God.
We've reached at long last the victor's goal,
But to keep the peace we must conquer the soul.
We have wrestled and vanquished the enemy,
But we enter a new Gethsemane.
The struggle now enters a realm deep within,
And each man has his own private battle to win. . .
And the words of Christ ring out in our ears
Amid the tumult of victory cheers,
And the Unknown Soldier pleads to be heard,
And his message is told in Christ's stirring words,
" 'Ye must be born again,' or we the slain
Have fought and fallen and died in vain."
Keep us grateful, omnipotent God,
And aware of those sleeping beneath the sod.
Strengthen our bonds with one another
So we may dwell as brother to brother.
Heal the wounds and be with us yet,
Lest we forget—lest we forget.

THE PRICELESS GIFT OF CHRISTMAS

Christmas is a heavenly gift that only God can give —
It's ours just for the asking
for as long as we shall live.
It can't be bought or bartered, it can't be won or sold,
It doesn't cost a penny, and it's worth
far more than gold.
It isn't bright and gleaming for eager eyes to see —
It can't be wrapped in tinsel
or placed beneath a tree. . . .
For the priceless gift of Christmas is meant just for the heart,
And we receive it only
when we become a part
Of the kingdom and the glory which
are ours to freely take,
For God sent the holy Christ child at
Christmas for our sake
So man might come to know Him and
feel His presence near
And see the many miracles performed
when He was here.
And this priceless gift of Christmas is
within the reach of all —
The rich, the poor, the young and old,
the greatest and the small.
So take His priceless gift of love —
reach out and you receive —
And the only payment that God asks
is just that you believe.

THE SPIRIT OF GIVING

Each year at Christmas, the spirit of giving
Adds joy to the season and gladness to living.
And knowing this happens when Christmas is here,
Why can't we continue throughout the year
To make our lives happy and abundant with living
By following each day the spirit of giving?

The Miracle of Christmas

The wonderment in a small child's eyes,
The ageless awe in the Christmas skies,
The nameless joy that fills the air,
The throngs that kneel in praise and prayer—
These are the things that make us know
That men may come and men may go,
But none will ever find a way
To banish Christ from Christmas Day,
For with each child there's born again
A mystery that baffles men.

The Christmas Story

A star in the sky, an angel's voice
Telling the world—Rejoice! Rejoice!
Shepherds tending their flocks by night,
Falling in awe at this wondrous sight;
Wise men traveling across the lands
To place their gifts in the Christ child's hands;
No room at the inn, so a manger bed
Cradled in radiance the holy babe's head. . .
That is the story that's living still
In the hearts of all men.

Behold, I Bring You Good Tidings of Great Joy

Glad tidings herald the Christ child's birth—
Joy to the world and peace on earth,
Glory to God. . .Let all men rejoice
And hearken once more to the angel's voice.
It matters not who or what you are—
All men can behold the Christmas star,
For the star that shone is shining still
In the hearts of men of peace and goodwill.
It offers the answer to every man's need,
Regardless of color or race or creed. . .
So joining together in brotherly love,
Let us worship again our Father above,
And forgetting our own little selfish desires,
May we seek what the star of Christmas inspires.

EVERYDAY
GLADNESS

A Sure Way to a Happy Day

Happiness is something we create in our minds;
It's not something you search for and so seldom find.
It's just waking up and beginning the day
By counting our blessings and kneeling to pray.
It's giving up thoughts that breed discontent
And accepting what comes as a gift heaven-sent.
It's giving up wishing for things we have not
And making the best of whatever we've got.
It's knowing that life is determined for us
And pursuing our tasks without fret, fume, or fuss. . .
For it's by completing what God gives us to do
That we find real contentment and happiness, too.

WHAT IS LIFE?

Life is a sojourn here on earth
Which begins the day God gives us birth.
We enter this world from the great unknown,
And God gives each spirit a form of its own
And endows this form with a heart and a soul
To spur man on to his ultimate goal. . .
And through the senses of feeling and seeing,
God makes man into a human being
So he may experience a mortal life
And through this period of smiles and strife
Prepare himself to return as he came,
For birth and death are in essence the same,
For both are fashioned by God's mighty hand,
And while we cannot understand,
We know we are born to die and arise,
For beyond this world in beauty lies
The purpose of living and the ultimate goal
God gives at birth to each seeking soul. . .
So enjoy your sojourn on earth and be glad
That God gives you a choice between
good things and bad,
And only be sure that you heed God's voice
Whenever life asks you to make a choice.

Live Lavishly!
Live Abundantly!

The more you give, the more you get;
The more you laugh, the less you fret.
The more you do unselfishly,
The more you live abundantly.
The more of everything you share,
The more you'll always have to spare.
The more you love, the more you'll find
That life is good and friends are kind,
For only what we give away
Enriches us from day to day.

Giving Is the Key to Living

Every day is a reason for giving
And giving is the key to living. . .
So let us give ourselves away
Not just today but every day.
And remember, a kind and thoughtful deed
Or a hand outstretched in a time of need
Is the rarest of gifts, for it is a part
Not of the purse but a loving heart. . .
And he who gives of himself will find
True joy of heart and peace of mind.

Heart Gifts

It's not the things that can be bought
That are life's richest treasures;
It's just the little "heart gifts"
That money cannot measure.
A cheerful smile, a friendly word,
A sympathetic nod,
All priceless little treasures
From the storehouse of our God.
They are the things that can't be bought
With silver or with gold,
For thoughtfulness and kindness
And love are never sold.
They are the priceless things in life
For which no one can pay,
And the giver finds rich recompense
In giving them away.

Take Time to Be Kind

Kindness is a virtue given by the Lord—
It pays dividends in happiness and joy is its reward.
For if you practice kindness in all you say and do,
The Lord will wrap His kindness around
your heart and you.

Be Glad

Be glad that your life has been full and complete;
Be glad that you've tasted the bitter and sweet.
Be glad that you've walked in sunshine and rain;
Be glad that you've felt both pleasure and pain.
Be glad that you've had such a full, happy life;
Be glad for your joy as well as your strife.
Be glad that you've walked with courage each day;
Be glad you've had strength for each step of the way.
Be glad for the comfort that you've found in prayer.
Be glad for God's blessings, His love, and His care.

LIFE

A little laughter, a little song,
A little teardrop
When things go wrong,
A little calm
And a little strife,
A little loving —
And that is life.

Where There Is Love

Where there is love the heart is light;
Where there is love the day is bright.
Where there is love there is a song
To help when things are going wrong.
Where there is love there is a smile
To make all things seem more worthwhile.
Where there is love there's a quiet peace,
A tranquil place where turmoils cease.
Love changes darkness into light
And makes the heart take wingless flight.
Oh, blessed are those who walk in love;
They also walk with God above.

Your Life Will Be Blessed If You Look for the Best

It's easy to grow downhearted
when nothing goes your way,
It's easy to be discouraged when
you have a troublesome day,
But trouble is only a challenge
to spur you on to achieve
The best that God has to offer,
if you have the faith to believe!

Inspiration! Meditation! Dedication!

Brighten your day
And lighten your way
And lessen your cares
With daily prayers.
Quiet your mind
And leave tension behind
And find inspiration
In hushed meditation.

If You Meet God in the Morning, He'll Go with You through the Day

The earth is the Lord's and the fullness thereof. . .
It speaks of His greatness, it sings of His love.
And each day at dawning I lift my heart high
And raise up my eyes to the infinite sky.
I watch the night vanish as a new day is born,
And I hear the birds sing on the wings of the morn.
I see the dew glisten in crystal-like splendor
While God, with a touch that is gentle and tender,
Wraps up the night and softly tucks it away
And hangs out the sun to herald a new day. . .
And so I give thanks and my heart kneels to pray,
"God, keep me and guide me and go with me today."

Seek Ye First the Kingdom of God

Life is a mixture of sunshine and rain,
Good things and bad things, pleasure and pain.
We can't have all sunshine, but it's certainly true
That there's never a cloud the sun
doesn't shine through. . .
So always remember, whatever betide you,
The power of God is always beside you. . .
And if friends disappoint you and plans go astray
And nothing works out in just the right way,
And you feel you have failed in achieving your goal
And that life wrongly placed you in an unfitting role,
Take heart and stand tall and think who you are,
For God is your Father and no one can bar
Or keep you from reaching your desired success
Or withhold the joy that is yours to possess. . .
For with God on your side, it matters not who
Is working to keep life's good things from you,
For you need nothing more than God's
guidance and love
To ensure you the things that you're most worthy of. . .
So trust in His wisdom and follow His ways
And be not concerned with the world's empty praise,
But first seek His kingdom and you will possess
The world's greatest of riches,
which is true happiness.

PRAYERS OF PRAISE

POWER OF PRAYER

I am only a worker employed by the Lord,
And great is my gladness and rich my reward
If I can just spread the wonderful story
That God is the answer to eternal glory. . .
Bringing new hope and comfort and cheer,
Telling sad hearts there is nothing to fear,
And what greater joy could there be than to share
The love of God and the power of prayer.

The Heavenly Staircase

Prayers are the stairs that lead to God,
And there's joy every step of the way
When we make our pilgrimage to
Him with love in our hearts each day.

Thank You, God, for Everything

Thank You, God, for everything—
the big things and the small—
For every good gift comes from God,
the Giver of them all,
And all too often we accept
without any thanks or praise
The gifts God sends as blessings
each day in many ways.
And so at this time we offer up a prayer
To thank You, God, for giving us
a lot more than our share.
First, thank You for the little things
that often come our way—
The things we take for granted and
don't mention when we pray—
Then thank You for the miracles
we are much too blind to see,
And give us new awareness of
our many gifts from Thee.
And help us to remember that
the key to life and living
Is to make each prayer a prayer of thanks
and each day a day of thanksgiving.

So Many Reasons to Love the Lord

Thank You, God, for little
things that come unexpectedly
To brighten up a dreary day
that dawned so dismally.
Thank You, God, for sending
a happy thought my way
To blot out my depression
on a disappointing day.
Thank You, God, for brushing the
dark clouds from my mind
And leaving only sunshine
and joy of heart behind.
Oh God, the list is endless of the
things to thank You for,
But I take them all for granted
and unconsciously ignore
That everything I think or do,
each movement that I make,
Each measured, rhythmic heartbeat,
each breath of life I take
Is something You have given me
for which there is no way
For me in all my smallness to in any way repay.

I Come to Meet You

I come to meet You, God, and as I linger here
I seem to feel You very near.
A rustling leaf, a rolling slope
Speak to my heart of endless hope.
The sun just rising in the sky,
The waking birdlings as they fly,
The grass all wet with morning dew
Are telling me I just met You. . .
And gently thus the day is born
As night gives way to breaking morn,
And once again I've met You, God,
And worshipped on Your holy sod. . .
For who could see the dawn break through
Without a glimpse of heaven and You?
For who but God could make the day
And softly put the night away?

Show Me the Way

Show me the way not to fortune and fame,
Not how to win laurels or praise for my name,
But show me the way to spread the great story
That Thine is the kingdom and power and glory.

God's Assurance Gives Us Endurance

My blessings are so many,
my troubles are so few,
How can I be discouraged when
I know that I have You?
And I have the sweet assurance
that there's nothing I need fear
If I but keep remembering I
am Yours and You are near.
Help me to endure the storms that
keep raging deep inside me,
And make me more aware each
day that no evil can betide me.
If I remain undaunted though
the billows sweep and roll,
Knowing I have Your assurance,
there's a haven for my soul,
For anything and everything
can somehow be endured
If Your presence is beside me
and lovingly assured.

No Favor Do I Seek Today

I come not to ask, to plead or implore You —
I just come to tell You how much I adore You.
For to kneel in Your presence makes me feel blessed,
For I know that You know all my needs best,
And it fills me with joy just to linger with You
As my soul You replenish and my heart You renew.
For prayer is much more than just asking for things —
It's the peace and contentment that quietness brings.
So thank You again for Your mercy and love
And for making me heir to Your kingdom above.

A Prayer of Thanks

Thank You, God, for the beauty
around me everywhere,
The gentle rain and glistening dew,
the sunshine and the air,
The joyous gift of feeling the soul's soft,
whispering voice
That speaks to me from deep within
and makes my heart rejoice.

Show Me More Clearly the Way to Serve and Love You More Each Day

God, help me in my feeble way
To somehow do something each day
To show You that I love You best
And that my faith will stand each test,
And let me serve You every day
And feel You near me when I pray.
Oh, hear my prayer, dear God above,
And make me worthy of Your love.

A Part of Me

Dear God, You are a part of me —
You're all I do and all I see;
You're what I say and what I do,
For all my life belongs to You.
You walk with me and talk with me,
For I am Yours eternally,
And when I stumble, slip, and fall
Because I'm weak and lost and small,
You help me up and take my hand
And lead me toward the Promised Land.
I cannot dwell apart from You —
You would not ask or want me to,
For You have room within Your heart
To make each child of Yours a part
Of You and all Your love and care
If we but come to You in prayer.

THE CALL TO REJOICE

Why Am I Complaining?

My cross is not too heavy,
my road is not too rough
Because God walks beside me,
and to know this is enough. . .
And though I get so lonely,
I know I'm not alone,
For the Lord God is my Father
and He loves me as His own. . .
So though I'm tired and weary
and I wish my race were run,
God will only terminate it when
my work on earth is done. . .
So let me stop complaining
about my load of care,
For God will always lighten it
when it gets too much to bear. . .
And if He does not ease my load,
He'll give me strength to bear it,
For God, in love and mercy,
is always near to share it.

On the Wings of Prayer

On the wings of prayer our burdens take flight
And our load of care becomes bearably light
And our heavy hearts are lifted above
To be healed by the balm of God's wonderful love. . .
And the tears in our eyes are dried by the hands
Of a loving Father who understands
All of our problems, our fears and despair,
When we take them to Him on the wings of prayer.

THE HOUSE OF PRAYER

Just close your eyes and open your heart
And feel your cares and worries depart.
Just yield yourself to the Father above
And let Him hold you secure in His love. . .
For life on earth grows more involved
With endless problems that can't be solved,
But God only asks us to do our best;
Then He will take over and finish the rest. . .
So when you are tired, discouraged, and blue,
There's always one door that is opened to you,
And that is the door to the house of prayer,
And you'll find God waiting to meet you there. . .
And the house of prayer is no farther away
Than the quiet spot where you kneel and pray.
For the heart is a temple when God is there
As we place ourselves in His loving care. . .
And He hears every prayer and answers each one
When we pray in His name, "Thy will be done."
And the burdens that seemed too heavy to bear
Are lifted away on the wings of prayer.

Now I Lay Me Down to Sleep

I remember so well this prayer I said
Each night as my mother tucked me in bed,
And today this same prayer is still the best way
To sign off with God at the end of the day
And to ask Him your soul to safely keep
As you wearily close your tired eyes in sleep,
Feeling content that the Father above
Will hold you secure in His great arms of love. . .
And having His promise that if ere you wake
His angels reach down, your sweet soul to take,
Is perfect assurance that, awake or asleep,
God is always right there to tenderly keep
All of His children ever safe in His care,
For God's here and He's there
and He's everywhere. . .
So into His hands each night as I sleep
I commend my soul for the dear Lord to keep,
Knowing that if my soul should take flight,
It will soar to the land where there is no night.

My Garden of Prayer

My garden beautifies my yard
and adds fragrance to the air,
But it is also my cathedral and
my quiet place of prayer.
So little do we realize that
the glory and the power
Of Him who made the universe
lie hidden in a flower!

God's Stairway

Step by step we climb day by day
Closer to God with each prayer we pray,
For the cry of the heart offered in prayer
Becomes just another spiritual stair
In the heavenly place where we live anew. . .
So never give up, for it's worth the climb
To live forever in endless time
Where the soul of man is safe and free
To live and love through eternity.

Anywhere Is a Place of Prayer If God Is There

I have prayed on my knees in the morning,
I have prayed as I walked along,
I have prayed in the silence and darkness,
and I've prayed to the tune of a song.
I have prayed in churches and chapels,
cathedrals and synagogues, too,
But often I had the feeling that my
prayers were not getting through. . .
And I realized then that our Father is
not really concerned when we pray
Or impressed by our manner of worship
or the eloquent words that we say.
He is only concerned with our feelings,
and He looks deep into our hearts
And hears the cry of our souls' deep need
that no words could ever impart. . .
So it isn't the prayer that's expressive
or offered in some special spot
That's the sincere plea of a sinner,
and God can tell whether or not
We honestly seek His forgiveness
and earnestly mean what we say,
And then and then only God answers
the prayers that we fervently pray.

Faith and Trust

Sometimes when a light
Goes out of our lives
And we are left in darkness
And we do not know which way to go,
We must put our hand
Into the hand of God
And ask Him to lead us.
And if we let our lives become a prayer
Until we are strong enough
To stand under the weight
Of our own thoughts again,
Somehow, even the most difficult
Hours are bearable.

Help Us to See and Understand

God, give us wider vision to see and understand
That both the sunshine and the showers
are gifts from Thy great hand,
And when our lives are overcast
with trouble and with care,
Give us faith to see beyond
the dark clouds of despair,
And teach us that it takes the showers
to make the flowers grow,
And only in the storms of life when
the winds of trouble blow
Can man, too, reach maturity and
grow in faith and grace
And gain the strength and courage
to enable him to face
Sunny days as well as rain,
high peaks as well as low,
Knowing that the April showers
will make May flowers grow. . .
And then at last may we accept the
sunshine and the showers,
Confident it takes them both
to make salvation ours.

TALK IT OVER WITH GOD

You're worried and troubled about everything,
Wondering and fearing what tomorrow will bring.
You long to tell someone, for you feel so alone,
But your friends are all burdened
with cares of their own.
There is only one place and only one Friend
Who is never too busy, and you can always depend
On Him to be waiting, with arms open wide
To hear all the troubles you came to confide. . .
For the heavenly Father will always be there
When you seek Him and find Him
at the altar of prayer.

LET DAILY PRAYER DISSOLVE YOUR CARES

We all have cares and problems
we cannot solve alone,
But if we go to God in prayer,
we are never on our own,
And no day is unmeetable if,
on rising, our first thought
Is to thank God for the blessings
that His loving care has brought,
For there can be no failures
or hopeless, unsaved sinners
If we enlist the help of God,
who makes all losers winners. . .
So meet Him in the morning
and go with Him through the day
And thank Him for His guidance
each evening when you pray,
And if you follow faithfully
this daily way to pray,
You will never in your lifetime
face another hopeless day. . .
For like a soaring eagle, you too can rise above
The storms of life around you on the
wings of prayer and love.

Finding Faith in a Flower

Sometimes when faith is running low
And I cannot fathom why things are so,
I walk among the flowers that grow
And learn the answers to all I would know. . .
For among my flowers I have come to see
Life's miracle and its mystery,
And standing in silence and reverie,
My faith comes flooding back to me.

How Great the Yield from a Fertile Field

The farmer plows through the fields of green,
And the blade of the plow is sharp and keen,
But the seed must be sown to bring forth grain,
For nothing is born without suffering and pain,
And God never plows in the soul of man
Without intention and purpose and plan. . .
So whenever you feel the plow's sharp blade,
Let not your heart be sorely afraid,
For like the farmer, God chooses a field
From which He expects an excellent yield. . .
So rejoice though your heart be broken in two—
God seeks to bring forth a rich harvest in you.

THE DELIGHTS OF
FRIENDSHIP

Discouragement and Dreams

So many things in the line of duty
Drain us of effort and leave us no beauty,
And the dust of the soul grows thick and unswept;
The spirit is drenched in tears unwept.
But just as we fall beside the road,
Discouraged with life and bowed down with our load,
We lift our eyes, and what seemed a dead end
Is the street of dreams where we meet a friend.

My God Is No Stranger

God is no stranger in a faraway place;
He's as close as the wind that blows 'cross my face.
It's true I can't see the wind as it blows,
But I feel it around me and my heart surely knows
That God's mighty hand can be felt everywhere,
For there's nothing on earth that is not in God's care.
The sky and the stars, the waves and the sea,
The dew on the grass, the leaves on a tree
Are constant reminders of God and His nearness,
Proclaiming His presence with crystal-like clearness.
So how could I think God was far, far away
When I feel Him beside me every hour of the day?
And I've plenty of reasons to know God's my friend,
And this is one friendship that time cannot end.

Life Is a Garden

Life is a garden, good friends are the flowers,
And times spent together life's happiest hours. . .
And friendship, like flowers, blooms ever more fair
When carefully tended by dear friends who care. . .

The Art of Greatness

It's not fortune or fame or worldwide acclaim
That makes for true greatness, you'll find;
It's the wonderful art of teaching the heart
To always be thoughtful and kind!

The Garden of Friendship

There is no garden
So complete
But roses could make
The place more sweet.
There is no life
So rich and rare
But one more friend
Could enter there.

Deep in My Heart

Happy little memories go
flitting through my mind,
And in all my thoughts and
memories I always seem to find
The picture of your face, dear,
the memory of your touch,
And all the other little things
I've come to love so much.
You cannot go beyond my thoughts
or leave my love behind,
Because I keep you in my heart
and forever on my mind. . .
And though I may not tell you,
I think you know it's true
That I find daily happiness in
the very thought of you.

FRIENDS ARE LIFE'S GIFT OF LOVE

If people like me didn't know people like you,
Life would lose its meaning and its richness, too. . .
For the friends that we make are life's gift of love,
And I think friends are sent right
from heaven above. . .
And thinking of you somehow makes me feel
That God is love and He's very real.

THE GIFT OF FRIENDSHIP

Friendship is a priceless gift that
cannot be bought or sold,
But its value is far greater than
a mountain made of gold—
For gold is cold and lifeless,
it can neither see nor hear,
And in the time of trouble
it is powerless to cheer.
It has no ears to listen,
no heart to understand;
It cannot bring you comfort
or reach out a helping hand—
So when you ask God for a gift,
be thankful if He sends
Not diamonds, pearls, or riches,
but the love of real true friends.

On Life's Busy Thoroughfares We Meet with Angels Unawares

The unexpected kindness from
an unexpected place,
A hand outstretched in friendship,
a smile on someone's face,
A word of understanding
spoken in a time of trial
Are unexpected miracles
that make life more worthwhile.
We know not how it happened
that in an hour of need
Somebody out of nowhere
proved to be a friend indeed. . .
For God has many messengers
we fail to recognize,
But He sends them when we need them,
and His ways are wondrous and wise. . .
So keep looking for an angel
and keep listening to hear,
For on life's busy, crowded streets,
you will find God's presence near.

A Friend Is a Gift from God

Among the great and glorious
gifts our heavenly Father sends
Is the gift of understanding that
we find in loving friends. . .
For somehow in the generous
heart of loving, faithful friends,
The good God in His charity
and wisdom always sends
A sense of understanding
and the power of perception
And mixes these fine qualities
with kindness and affection. . .
So when we need some sympathy
or a friendly hand to touch
Or one who listens tenderly and
speaks words that mean so much,
We seek a true and trusted friend
in the knowledge that we'll find
A heart that's sympathetic
and an understanding mind. . .
And often just without a word
there seems to be a union
Of thoughts and kindred feelings,
for God gives true friends communion.

BLESSINGS FROM ABOVE

*S*HOWERS OF BLESSINGS

Each day there are showers of
blessings sent from the Father above,
For God is a great, lavish giver,
and there is no end to His love. . .
And His grace is more than sufficient,
His mercy is boundless and deep,
And His infinite blessings are countless,
and all this we're given to keep
If we but seek God and find Him
and ask for a bounteous measure
Of this wholly immeasurable offering
from God's inexhaustible treasure. . .
For no matter how big man's dreams are,
God's blessings are infinitely more,
For always God's giving is greater
than what man is asking for.

Into our lives come many things
to break the dull routine —
The things we had not planned
on that happen unforeseen,
The unexpected little joys that
are scattered on our way,
Success we did not count on
or a rare, fulfilling day,
The sudden, unplanned meeting
that comes with sweet surprise
And lights the heart with happiness
like a rainbow in the skies.
Now some folks call it fickle fate
and some folks call it chance,
While others just accept it
as a pleasant happenstance.
But no matter what you call it,
it didn't come without design,
For all our lives are fashioned
by the hand that is divine,
And every lucky happening and
every lucky break
Are little gifts from God above
that are ours to freely take.

BLESSINGS DEVISED BY GOD

God speaks to us in many ways,
Altering our lives, our plans, and our days,
And His blessings come in many guises
That He alone in love devises,
And sorrow, which we dread so much,
Can bring a very healing touch. . .
For when we fail to heed His voice
We leave the Lord no other choice
Except to use a firm, stern hand
To make us know He's in command. . .
For on the wings of loss and pain,
The peace we often sought in vain
Will come to us with sweet surprise,
For God is merciful and wise. . .
And through dark hours of tribulation
God gives us time for meditation,
And nothing can be counted loss
Which teaches us to bear our cross.

EXPECTATION! ANTICIPATION! REALIZATION!

God gives us a power we so seldom employ,
For we're so unaware it is filled with such joy.
The gift that God gives us is anticipation,
Which we can fulfill with sincere expectation,
For there's power in belief when we think we will find
Joy for the heart and peace for the mind,
And believing the day will bring a surprise
Is not only pleasant but surprisingly wise. . .
For we open the door to let joy walk through
When we learn to expect the best and the most, too,
And believing we'll find a happy surprise
Makes reality out of a fancied surmise.

The Blessings of Sharing

Only what we give away
Enriches us from day to day,
For not in getting but in giving
Is found the lasting joy of living.
For no one ever had a part
In sharing treasures of the heart
Who did not feel the impact of
The magic mystery of God's love.
And love alone can make us kind
And give us joy and peace of mind,
So live with joy unselfishly
And you'll be blessed abundantly.

Motherhood

The dearest gifts that heaven
holds, the very finest, too,
Were made into one pattern that
was perfect, sweet, and true.
The angels smiled, well pleased,
and said, "Compared to all the others,
This pattern is so wonderful
let's use it just for mothers!"
And through the years, a mother
has been all that's sweet and good,
For there's a bit of God and love
in all true motherhood.

THERE ARE BLESSINGS IN EVERYTHING

Blessings come in many guises
That God alone in love devises,
And sickness, which we dread so much,
Can bring a very healing touch,
For often on the wings of pain
The peace we sought before in vain
Will come to us with sweet surprise,
For God is merciful and wise. . .
And through long hours of tribulation
God gives us time for meditation,
And no sickness can be counted loss
That teaches us to bear our cross.

A Time of Renewal
and Spiritual Blessing

No one likes to be sick and yet we know
It takes sunshine and rain to make flowers grow,
And if we never were sick and we never felt pain,
We'd be like a desert without any rain,
And who wants a life that is barren and dry
With never a cloud to darken the sky?
For continuous sun goes unrecognized
Like the blessings God sends,
which are often disguised,
For sometimes a sickness that seems so distressing
Is a time of renewal and spiritual blessing.

Things to Be Thankful For

The good green earth beneath our feet,
The air we breathe, the food we eat,
Some work to do, a goal to win,
A hidden longing deep within
That spurs us on to bigger things
And helps us meet what each day brings—
All these things and many more
Are things we should be thankful for. . .
And most of all, our thankful prayers
Should rise to God because He cares.

Beyond Our Asking

More than hearts can imagine or minds comprehend,
God's bountiful gifts are ours without end.
We ask for a cupful when the vast sea is ours,
We pick a small rosebud from a garden of flowers,
We reach for a sunbeam but the sun still abides,
We draw one short breath but there's air on all sides.
Whatever we ask for falls short of God's giving,
For His greatness exceeds every facet of living,
And always God's ready and eager and willing
To pour out His mercy, completely fulfilling
All of man's needs for peace, joy, and rest,
For God gives His children whatever is best.
Just give Him a chance to open His treasures,
And He'll fill your life with unfathomable pleasures—
Pleasures that never grow worn out and faded
And leave us depleted, disillusioned, and jaded—
For God has a storehouse just filled to the brim
With all that man needs if we'll only ask Him.

MEMORIES

Tender little memories
Of some word or deed
Give us strength and courage
When we are in need.
Blessed little memories
Help us bear the cross
And soften all the bitterness
Of failure and loss.
Precious little memories
Of little things we've done
Make the very darkest day
A bright and happy one.

The Happiness You Already Have

Memories are treasures
that time cannot destroy;
They are the happy pathway
to yesterday's bright joy.

A Thankful Heart

Take nothing for granted, for whenever you do,
The joy of enjoying is lessened for you.
For we rob our own lives much more than we know
When we fail to respond or in any way show
Our thanks for the blessings that daily are ours—
The warmth of the sun, the fragrance of flowers,
The beauty of twilight, the freshness of dawn,
The coolness of dew on a green velvet lawn,
The kind little deeds so thoughtfully done,
The favors of friends and the love that someone
Unselfishly gives us in a myriad of ways,
Expecting no payment and no words of praise.
Oh, great is our loss when we no longer find
A thankful response to things of this kind.
For the joy of enjoying and the fullness of living
Are found in the heart that is filled
with thanksgiving.

REFLECTIONS ON
GOD'S LOVE

God's Love Is a Haven
in the Storms of Life

God's love is like an island
in life's ocean—vast and wide,
A peaceful, quiet shelter from
the restless, rising tide.
God's love is like a fortress,
and we seek protection there
When the waves of tribulation
seem to drown us in despair.
God's love is a sanctuary where
our souls can find sweet rest
From the struggle and the tension
of life's fast and futile quest.
God's love is like a tower rising
far above the crowd,
And God's smile is like the sunshine breaking
through the threatening cloud.
God's love is like a beacon burning
bright with faith and prayer,
And through all the changing scenes of life,
we can find a haven there.
For God's love is fashioned
after something enduring,
And it is endless and unfailing
like His character above.

TRUST GOD

Take heart and meet each minute
with faith in God's great love,
Aware that every day of life
is controlled by God above. . .
And never dread tomorrow
or what the future brings—
Just pray for strength and courage
and trust God in all things.

$\mathcal{W}$INGS OF LOVE

The priceless gift of life is love,
For with the help of God above
Love can change the human race
And make this world a better place. . .
For love dissolves all hate and fear
And makes our vision bright and clear
So we can see and rise above
Our pettiness on wings of love.

Never Be Discouraged

There is really nothing we need
know or even try to understand
If we refuse to be discouraged
and trust God's guiding hand,
So take heart and meet each minute
with faith in God's great love,
Aware that every day of life
is controlled by God above.
And never dread tomorrow
or what the future brings;
Just pray for strength and courage
and trust God in all things,
And never grow discouraged —
be patient and just wait,
For God never comes too early,
and He never comes too late.

Stepping Stones to God

An aching heart is but a stepping stone
To greater joy than you've ever known,
For things that cause the heart to ache
Until you think that it must break
Become the strength by which we climb
To higher heights that are sublime
And feel the radiance of God's smiles
When we have soared above life's trials.
So when you're overwhelmed with fears
And all your hopes are drenched in tears,
Think not that life has been unfair
And given you too much to bear,
For God has chosen you because,
With all your weaknesses and flaws,
He feels that you are worthy of
The greatness of His wondrous love.

Do Not Be Anxious

Do not be anxious, said our Lord,
Have peace from day to day—
The lilies neither toil nor spin,
Yet none are clothed as they.
The meadowlark with sweetest song
Fears not for bread or nest
Because he trusts our Father's love
And God knows what is best.

The Magic of Love

Love is like magic and it always will be,
For love still remains life's sweet mystery.
Love works in ways that are wondrous and strange,
And there's nothing in life that love cannot change.
Love can transform the most commonplace
Into beauty and splendor and sweetness and grace.
Love is unselfish, understanding, and kind,
For it sees with its heart and not with its mind.
Love gives and forgives; there is nothing too much
For love to heal with its magic touch.
Love is the language that every heart speaks,
For love is the one thing that every heart seeks. . .
And where there is love, God, too, will abide
And bless the family residing inside.

God Is Never beyond Our Reach

No one ever sought the Father
and found He was not there,
And no burden is too heavy
to be lightened by a prayer.
No problem is too intricate,
and no sorrow that we face
Is too deep and devastating to
be softened by His grace.
No trials and tribulations are
beyond what we can bear
If we share them with our Father
as we talk to Him in prayer. . .
God asks for no credentials —
He accepts us with our flaws.
He is kind and understanding
and He welcomes us because
We are His erring children
and He loves us, every one,
And He freely and completely
forgives all that we have done,
Asking only if we're ready
to follow where He leads,
Content that in His wisdom
He will answer all our needs.

He Loves You

It's amazing and incredible,
but it's as true as it can be—
God loves and understands us all,
and that means you and me.
His grace is all-sufficient for
both the young and old,
For the lonely and the timid,
for the brash and for the bold.
His love knows no exceptions,
so never feel excluded;
No matter who or what you are,
your name has been included. . .
And no matter what your past has been,
trust God to understand,
And no matter what your problem is,
just place it in His hand. . .
For in all our unloveliness this
great God loves us still—
He loved us since the world began,
and what's more, He always will!

God Loves Us

We are all God's children and
He loves us, every one.
He freely and completely
forgives all that we have done,
Asking only if we're ready to
follow where He leads,
Content that in His wisdom
He will answer all our needs.

Blessings in Disguise
Are Difficult to Recognize

God sends His little angels in many forms and guises.
They come as lovely miracles that God alone devises,
For He does nothing without purpose;
everything's a perfect plan
To fulfill in bounteous measure
all He ever promised man. . .
For every little angel with a body bent or broken
Or a little mind challenged or little words unspoken
Is just God's way of trying to reach
out and touch the hands
Of all who do not know Him and cannot understand
That often through an angel whose
wings will never fly,
The Lord is pointing out the way to His eternal sky,
Where there will be no handicaps of
body, soul, or mind
And where all limitations will be
dropped and left behind. . .
So accept these little angels as gifts from God above,
And thank Him for this lesson in
faith and hope and love.

The Hand of God
Is Everywhere

It's true we have never looked on His face,
But His likeness shines forth from every place,
For the hand of God is everywhere
Along life's busy thoroughfare,
And His presence can be felt and seen
Right in the midst of our daily routine.
Things we touch and see and feel
Are what make God so very real.

Love One Another
As I Have Loved You

"Love one another as I have loved you"
May seem impossible to do,
But if you will try to trust and believe,
Great are the joys that you will receive
For love makes us patient, understanding, and kind,
And we judge with our hearts and not with our minds,
For as soon as love entered the heart's open door,
The faults we once saw are not there anymore
And the things that seem wrong begin to look right
When viewed in the softness of love's gentle light
For love works in ways that are wondrous and strange,
And there is nothing in life that love cannot change,
And all that God promised will someday come true
When you love one another the way He loved you.

HAPPINESS IN
ALL SEASONS

The Soul, Like Nature, Has Seasons, Too

When you feel cast down and despondently sad
And you long to be happy and carefree and glad,
Do you ask yourself, as I so often do,
Why must there be days that are cheerless and blue?
Why is the song silenced in the heart that was gay?
And then I ask God what makes life this way,
And His explanation makes everything clear—
The soul has its seasons the same as the year.
Man, too, must pass through life's autumn of death
And have his heart frozen by winter's cold breath,
But spring always comes with new life and birth,
Followed by summer to warm the soft earth. . .
And oh, what a comfort to know there are reasons
That souls, like nature, must too have their seasons—
Bounteous seasons and barren ones, too,
Times for rejoicing and times to be blue. . .
For with nothing but sameness how dull life would be,
For only life's challenge can set the soul free. . .
And it takes a mixture of both bitter and sweet
To season our lives and make them complete.

God's Unfailing Birthday Promise

From one birthday to another
God will gladly give
To everyone who seeks Him
and tries each day to live
A little bit more closely
to God and to each other,
Seeing everyone who passes as
a neighbor, friend, or brother,
Not only joy and happiness
but the faith to meet each trial
Not with fear and trepidation
but with an inner smile. . .
For we know life's never measured
by how many years we live
But by the kindly things we do
and the happiness we give.

After the Winter
God Sends the Spring

Springtime is a season
of hope and joy and cheer—
There's beauty all around us
to see and touch and hear. . .
So no matter how downhearted
and discouraged we may be,
New hope is born when we
behold leaves budding on a tree
Or when we see a timid flower
push through the frozen sod
And open wide in glad surprise
its petaled eyes to God. . .
For this is just God saying,
"Lift up your eyes to Me,
And the bleakness of your spirit,
like the budding springtime tree,
Will lose its wintry darkness
and your heavy heart will sing."
For God never sends the winter
without the joy of spring.

The Autumn of Life

What a wonderful time is life's autumn,
when the leaves of the trees are all gold,
When God fills each day as He sends it
with memories priceless and old.
What a treasure house filled with rare jewels
are the blessings of year upon year,
When life has been lived as you've lived it
in a home where God's presence is near. . .
May the deep meaning surrounding this day,
like the paintbrush of God up above,
Touch your life with wonderful blessings,
and fill your heart brimful with His love.

$\mathcal{E}$ACH SPRING GOD RENEWS HIS PROMISE

Long, long ago in a land far away,
There came the dawn of the first Easter day,
And each year we see the promise reborn
That God gave the world on that first Easter morn.
For in each waking flower and each singing bird
The promise of Easter is witnessed and heard,
And spring is God's way of speaking to men
And renewing the promise of Easter again. . .
For death is a season that man must pass through,
And just like the flowers, God wakens him, too.
So why should we grieve when our loved ones die,
For we'll meet them again in a cloudless sky.
For Easter is more than a beautiful story—
It's the promise of life and eternal glory.

APRIL

April comes with cheeks a-glowing
Silver streams are all a-flowing,
Flowers open wide their eyes
In lovely rapturous surprise.
Lilies dream beside the brooks,
Violets in meadow nooks,
And the birds gone wild with glee
Fill the woods with melody.

Everywhere across the Land You See God's Face and Touch His Hand

Each time you look up in the sky,
Or watch the fluffy clouds drift by,
Or feel the sunshine, warm and bright,
Or watch the dark night turn to light,
Or hear a bluebird brightly sing,
Or see the winter turn to spring,
Or stop to pick a daffodil,
Or gather violets on some hill,
Or touch a leaf or see a tree,
It's all God whispering, "This is Me. . .
And I am faith and I am light
And in Me there shall be no night."

Nothing Is Lost Forever

The waking earth in springtime
reminds us it is true
That nothing ever really dies
that is not born anew. . .
So trust God's all-wise wisdom
and doubt the Father never,
For in His heavenly kingdom
there is nothing lost forever.

THERE IS NO DEATH

There is no night without a dawning,
no winter without a spring,
And beyond death's dark horizon
our hearts once more will sing.
For those who leave us for a
while have only gone away
Out of a restless, careworn world
into a brighter day
Where there will be no partings
and time is not counted by years,
Where there are no trials or troubles,
no worries, no cares, and no tears.

Life's Golden Autumn

Memory opens wide the door
on a happy day like this,
And with a sweet nostalgia
we longingly recall,
The happy days of long ago
that seem the best of all. . .
But time cannot be halted in
its swift and endless flight,
And age is sure to follow youth
as day comes after night,
And once again it's proven that
the restless brain of man
Is powerless to alter God's great,
unchanging plan. . .
But while our steps grow slower
and we grow more tired, too,
The soul goes roaring upward
to realms untouched and new.

In God's Tomorrow There Is Eternal Spring

All nature heeds the call of spring
as God awakens everything,
And all that seemed so dead and still
experiences a sudden thrill
As springtime lays a magic hand
across God's vast and fertile land.
Oh, the joy in standing by
to watch a sapphire springtime sky
Or see a fragile flower break through
what just a day ago or two
Seemed barren ground still hard with frost,
for in God's world, no life is lost,
And flowers sleep beneath the ground,
but when they hear spring's waking sound,
They push themselves through layers of clay
to reach the sunlight of God's day.
And man and woman, like flowers, too, must sleep
until called from the darkened deep
To live in that place where angels sing
and where there is eternal spring.

ᏗHE GOLDEN YEARS OF LIFE

God in His loving and all-wise way
Makes the heart that once was too young yesterday
Serene and more gentle and less restless, too,
Content to remember the joys it once knew. . .
And all that we sought on the pathway of pleasure
Becomes but a memory to cherish and treasure—
The fast pace grows slower and the spirit serene,
And our souls can envision what
our eyes have not seen. . .
And so, while life's springtime is sweet to recall,
The autumn of life is the best time of all,
For our wild, youthful yearnings all gradually cease
And God fills our days with beauty and peace!

ALL NATURE PROCLAIMS
ETERNAL LIFE

Flowers sleeping 'neath the snow,
Awakening when the spring winds blow,
Leafless trees so bare before
Gowned in lacy green once more,
Hard, unyielding, frozen sod
Now softly carpeted by God,
Still streams melting in the spring,
Rippling over rocks that sing,
Barren, windswept, lonely hills
Turning gold with daffodils—
These miracles are all around
Within our sight and touch and sound,
As true and wonderful today
As when the stone was rolled away,
Proclaiming to all doubting men
That in God all things live again.

THE MYSTERY AND MIRACLE OF HIS CREATIVE HAND

In the beauty of a snowflake
falling softly on the land
Is the mystery and the miracle
of God's great, creative hand.
What better answers are there
to prove His holy being
Than the wonders all around us
that are ours just for the seeing?

UPLIFTING OPTIMISM

It's a Wonderful World

In spite of the fact we complain and lament
And view this old world with much discontent,
Deploring conditions and grumbling because
There's so much injustice and so many flaws,
It's a wonderful world, and it's people like you
Who make it that way by the things that they do.
For a warm, ready smile or a kind, thoughtful deed
Or a hand outstretched in an hour of need
Can change our whole outlook
and make the world bright
Where a minute before just nothing seemed right.
It's a wonderful world and it always will be
If we keep our eyes open and focused to see
The wonderful things man is capable of
When he opens his heart to God and His love.

Yesterday, Today, and Tomorrow

Yesterday's dead, tomorrow's unborn,
So there's nothing to fear and nothing to mourn,
For all that is past and all that has been
Can never return to be lived once again. . .
And what lies ahead or the things that will be
Are still in God's hands, so it is not up to me
To live in the future that is God's great unknown,
For the past and the present God claims for His own. . .
So all I need do is to live for today
And trust God to show me the truth and the way.
For it's only the memory of things that have been
And expecting tomorrow to bring trouble again
That fills my today, which God wants to bless,
With uncertain fears and borrowed distress. . .
For all I need live for is this one little minute,
For life's here and now and eternity's in it.

Life's Disappointments Are God's Sweetest Appointments

Out of life's misery born of man's sins,
A fuller, richer life begins,
For when we are helpless with no place to go
And our hearts are heavy and our spirits are low,
If we place our lives in God's hands
And surrender completely to His will and demands,
The darkness lifts and the sun shines through,
And by His touch we are born anew.
So praise God for trouble that cuts like a knife
And disappointments that shatter your life,
For with patience to wait and faith to endure,
Your life will be blessed and your future secure.
For God is but testing your faith and your love
Before He appoints you to rise far above
All the small things that so sorely distress you,
For God's only intention is to strengthen and bless you.

$\mathscr{P}$ATIENCE

Most of the battles of life are won
By looking beyond the clouds to the sun
And having the patience to wait for the day
When the sun comes out and the clouds float away.

My Birthday in Bethseda

How little we know what God has in store
As daily He blesses our lives more and more.
I've lived many years and I've learned many things,
But today I have grown new spiritual wings. . .
For pain has a way of broadening our view
And bringing us closer in sympathy, too,
To those who are living in constant pain
And trying somehow to bravely sustain
The faith and endurance to keep on trying
When they almost welcome the peace of dying. . .
Without this experience I would have lived and died
Without fathoming the pain of Christ crucified,
For none of us knows what pain is all about
Until our spiritual wings start to sprout.
So thank You, God, for the gift You sent
To teach me that pain's heaven-sent.

THY WILL BE DONE

God did not promise sun without rain,
Light without darkness, or joy without pain.
He only promised strength for the day
When the darkness comes and we lose our way. . .
For only through sorrow do we grow more aware
That God is our refuge in times of despair.
For when we are happy and life's bright and fair,
We often forget to kneel down in prayer. . .
But God seems much closer and needed much more
When trouble and sorrow stand outside our door,
For then we seek shelter in His wondrous love,
And we ask Him to send us help from above. . .
And that is the reason we know it is true
That bright, shining hours and dark, sad ones, too,
Are part of the plan God made for each one,
And all we can pray is "Thy will be done."
And know that you are never alone,
For God is your Father and you're one of His own.

$\mathcal{S}$OMEBODY LOVES YOU

Somebody loves you more than you know,
Somebody goes with you wherever you go,
Somebody really and truly cares
And lovingly listens to all of your prayers. . .
Don't doubt for a minute that this is not true,
For God loves His children and
takes care of them, too. . .
And all of His treasures are yours to share
If you love Him completely and
show that you care. . .
And if you walk in His footsteps
and have faith to believe,
There's nothing you ask for that you will not receive!

$\mathcal{T}$HERE'S THE RAINBOW OF HOPE

The rainbow is God's promise
of hope for you and me,
And though the clouds hang heavy
and the sun we cannot see,
We know above the dark clouds
that fill the stormy sky
Hope's rainbow will come shining through
when the clouds have drifted by.

On the Other Side of Death

Death is a gateway we all must pass through
To reach that fair land where the soul's born anew,
For man's born to die, and his sojourn on earth
Is a short span of years beginning with birth.
And like pilgrims we wander until death takes our hand
And we start on the journey to God's Promised Land,
A place where we'll find no suffering or tears,
Where time is not counted in days, months, or years.
And in that fair city that God has prepared
Are unending joys to be happily shared
With all of our loved ones who patiently wait
On death's other side to open the gate.

The Home Beyond

We feel so sad when those we love
Are called to live in the home above,
But why should we grieve when they say good-bye
And go to dwell in a cloudless sky?
For they have but gone to prepare the way,
And we'll meet them again some happy day,
For God has told us that nothing can sever
A life He created to live forever.
So let God's promise soften our sorrow
And give us new strength for a brighter tomorrow.

Growing Older Is Part of God's Plan

You can't hold back the dawn
or stop the tides from flowing
Or keep a rose from withering
or still a wind that's blowing,
And time cannot be halted in
its swift and endless flight,
For age is sure to follow youth
like day comes after night. . .
For He who sets our span of years
and watches from above
Replaces youth and beauty with
peace and truth and love,
And then our souls are privileged
to see a hidden treasure
That in youth escapes our eyes
in our pursuit of pleasure. . .
So passing years are but blessings
that open up the way
To the everlasting beauty
of God's eternal day.

Make Your Day Bright by Thinking Right and Your Life Will Be Blessed If You Look for the Best

Don't start your day by supposin'
that trouble is just ahead;
It's better to stop supposin'
and start with a prayer instead. . .
And make it a prayer of thanksgiving for the
wonderful things God has wrought,
Like the beautiful sunrise and sunset,
God's gifts that are free and not bought. . .
For what is the use of supposin'
that dire things could happen to you,
Worrying about some misfortune
that seldom if ever comes true. . .
But instead of just idle supposin',
step forward to meet each new day
Secure in the knowledge God's near
you to lead you each step of the way. . .
So if you desire to be happy and
get rid of the misery of dread,
Just give up supposin' the worst things
and look for the best things instead.

Spring Awakens What Autumn Puts to Sleep

A garden of asters in varying hues,
Crimson pinks and violet blues,
Blossoming in the hazy fall,
Wrapped in autumn's lazy pall. . .
But early frost stole in one night,
And like a chilling, killing blight,
It touched each pretty aster's head,
And now the garden's still and dead,
And all the lovely flowers that bloomed
Will soon be buried and entombed
In winter's icy shroud of snow. . .
But oh, how wonderful to know
That after winter comes the spring
To breathe new life in everything,
And all the flowers that fell in death
Will be awakened by spring's breath. . .
For in God's plan both men and flowers
Can only reach bright, shining hours
By dying first to rise in glory
And prove again the Easter story.

BRIGHTEN THE CORNER
WHERE YOU ARE

It's not the big celebrity in
a world of fame and praise,
But it's doing unpretentiously
in undistinguished ways
The work that God assigned to us,
unimportant as it seems,
That makes our task outstanding
and brings reality to dreams. . .
So do not sit and idly wish for
wider, new dimensions
Where you can put in practice
your many good intentions,
But at the spot God placed you,
begin at once to do
Little things to brighten up the
lives surrounding you. . .
For if everybody brightened up the
spot on which they're standing
By being more considerate
and a little less demanding,
This dark old world would very
soon eclipse the evening star.
If everybody brightened up
the corner where they are.

Count Your Gains, and Not Losses

As we travel down life's busy road
Complaining of our heavy load,
We often think God's been unfair
And given us much more than our share
Of daily little irritations
And disappointing tribulations.
The good things we forget completely,
When God looked down and blessed us sweetly.
Our troubles fill our every thought,
We dwell upon the goals we sought,
And wrapped up in our own despair,
We have no time to see or share
Another's load that far outweighs
Our little problems and dismays. . .
And so we walk with heads held low,
And little do we guess or know
That someone near us on life's street
Is burdened deeply with defeat,
And if we'd but forget our care
And stop in sympathy to share
The burden that our brother carried,
Our minds and hearts would be less harried
And we would feel our load was small —
In fact, we carried no load at all.

Slowing Down

My days are so crowded and my hours so few
And I can no longer work fast like I used to do.
But I know I must learn to be satisfied
That God has not completely denied
The joy of working—at a much slower pace—
For as long as He gives me a little place
To work with Him in His vineyard of love,
Just to know that He's helping me from above
Gives me strength to meet each day
As I travel along life's changing way.

Look on the Sunny Side

There are always two sides—the good and the bad,
The dark and the light, the sad and the glad. . .
But in looking back over the good and the bad,
We're aware of the number of good things we've had,
And in counting our blessings,
we find when we're through
We've no reason at all to complain or be blue. . .
So thank God for the good things
He has already done,
And be grateful to Him for the battles you've won,
And know that the same God who helped you before
Is ready and willing to help you once more.
Then with faith in your heart,
reach out for God's hand
And accept what He sends,
though you can't understand. . .
For our Father in heaven always knows what is best,
And if you trust His wisdom,
your life will be blessed. . .
For always remember that whatever betide you,
You are never alone, for God is beside you.

Lives Distressed
Cannot Be Blessed

Refuse to be discouraged,
refuse to be distressed,
For when we are despondent,
our lives cannot be blessed.
For doubt and fear and worry
close the door to faith and prayer,
And there's no room for blessings
when we're lost in deep despair.
So remember when you're troubled
with uncertainty and doubt,
It is best to tell our Father
what our fear is all about,
For unless we seek His guidance
when troubled times arise,
We are bound to make decisions
that are twisted and unwise.
But when we view our problems
through the eyes of God above,
Misfortunes turn to blessings
and hatred turns to love.

This Is Just a Resting Place

Sometimes the road of life seems
long as we travel through the years,
And with hearts that are broken
and eyes brimful of tears,
We falter in our weariness
and sink beside the way,
But God leans down and whispers,
"Child, there'll be another day,"
And the road will grow much
smoother and much easier to face,
So do not be disheartened;
this is just a resting place.

Meet Life's Trials with Smiles

There are times when life overwhelms us
and our trials seem too many to bear;
It is then we should stop to remember
God is standing by ready to share
The uncertain hours that confront us
and fill us with fear and despair,
For God in His goodness has promised
that the cross that He gives us to wear
Will never exceed our endurance
or be more than our strength can bear. . .
And secure in that blessed assurance,
we can smile as we face tomorrow,
For God holds the key to the future,
and no sorrow or care we need borrow.

Be of Good Cheer, There's Nothing to Fear

Cheerful thoughts, like sunbeams,
lighten up the darkest fears,
For when the heart is happy
there's just no time for tears,
And when the face is smiling
it's impossible to frown,
And when you are high-spirited
you cannot feel low-down. . .
For the nature of our attitudes
toward circumstantial things
Determines our acceptance of
the problems that life brings,
And if you'll only try it,
you will find, without a doubt,
A cheerful attitude's something
no one should be without.
For when the heart is cheerful,
it cannot be filled with fear,
And without fear, the way ahead
seems more distinct and clear,
And we realize there's nothing
that we must face alone,
For our heavenly Father loves us,
and our problems are His own.

Burdens Can Be Blessings

Our Father knows what's best for us,
So why should we complain—
We always want the sunshine,
But He knows there must be rain.
We love the sound of laughter
And the merriment of cheer,
But our hearts would lose their tenderness
If we never shed a tear. . .
So whenever we are troubled
And life has lost its song,
It's God testing us with burdens
Just to make our spirit strong!

Conclusion

And now that you've come to the end of this book,
Pause and reflect and take a swift backward look
And you'll find that to follow God's
commandment each day
Is not only the righteous and straight, narrow way,
But a joyous experience, for there's many a thrill
In going God's way and in doing His will. . .
For in traveling God's way you are never alone,
For all of your problems God takes as His own,
And always He's ready to counsel and guide you,
And in sadness or gladness He's always beside you. . .
And to live for God's glory and to walk in His truth
Brings peace to the angel and joy to the youth,
And at the end of life's journey,
there's His promised reward
Of life everlasting in the house of the Lord.

INDEX